WORLD WAR II
EARLY BATTLES

BY JOHN HAMILTON

VISIT US AT
WWW.ABDOPUBLISHING.COM

Published by ABDO Publishing Company, 8000 West 78th Street, Suite 310, Edina, MN 55439. Copyright ©2012 by Abdo Consulting Group, Inc. International copyrights reserved in all countries. No part of this book may be reproduced in any form without written permission from the publisher. ABDO & Daughters™ is a trademark and logo of ABDO Publishing Company.

Printed in the United States of America, North Mankato, Minnesota.
082011
092011

 PRINTED ON RECYCLED PAPER

Editor: Sue Hamilton
Graphic Design: John Hamilton
Cover Design: Neil Klinepier
Cover Photo: National Archives and Records Administration (NARA)
Interior Photos and Illustrations: Corbis-pgs 8, 11, 22-23 & 29; Getty Images-pgs 5, 13 (inset left), 15 (inset left), 17 (inset right), 18 (top) & 19; Granger Collection-pgs 1, 6, 7, 9, 10, 12-13, 13 (inset right), 14-15, 16-17, 20-21, 21 (inset), 24-25 & 27; iStock-pgs 22 & 25 (maps); John Hamilton-pgs 4, 11, 18, 22, 25 & 28; NARA-pgs 3, 15 & 17 (inset left); *The New York Times*-pg 26; U.S. Navy-pg 25.

ABDO Booklinks

To learn more about World War II, visit ABDO Publishing Company online. Web sites about World War II are featured on our Book Links pages. These links are routinely monitored and updated to provide the most current information available. Web site: www.abdopublishing.com

Library of Congress Cataloging-in-Publication Data

Hamilton, John, 1959-
  World War II : early battles / John Hamilton.
    p. cm. -- (World War II)
  Includes index.
  ISBN 978-1-61783-059-4
  1. World War, 1939-1945--Juvenile literature. 2. Battles--History--20th century--Juvenile literature. I. Title.
  D743.7.H364 2012
  940.54'2--dc23
                    2011020133

CONTENTS

German troops parade through Warsaw, Poland, in September 1939.

THE PATH TO WAR

World War II was the deadliest struggle in human history. Whole countries were reduced to rubble. Nobody knows exactly how many people were killed, but at least 50 to 70 million lost their lives.

The aggressive policies of three countries were most responsible for starting World War II. They included Germany, Italy, and Japan. These countries formed an alliance called the Axis.

What caused World War II? In many ways, it was a continuation of an earlier war, World War I (1914-1918). That horrible conflict, the "war to end all wars," left Europe divided and weak. This sowed the seeds for World War II, an even bigger catastrophe to come.

Many countries had their borders redrawn after World War I. Germany lost much of its land to the victors.

Rubble fills the streets of London, England, after a German air raid in May 1941.

Benito Mussolini speaks in Rome in the 1930s. The Italian leader was part of the Fascist Party. He promised Italian citizens a strong, effective government.

In Italy, Benito Mussolini and the Fascist Party promised a strong, effective government and a rebirth of Italian glory.

In Asia, a newly industrialized and aggressive Japan began looking for ways to extend its power and resources, even if it meant invading its neighbors.

In Germany, the Nazi Party's Adolf Hitler tapped into people's resentment over the country's mistreatment at the end of World War I. Largely because of the Versailles Treaty, Germany was left with crushing inflation and unemployment. One out of three workers were without jobs.

Many Germans hoped their country could somehow regain its past greatness. Hitler and the Nazis were determined to make that dream come true, even if it meant war. Within a year of coming to power in 1933, Hitler stamped out all political resistance inside Germany. He rapidly built a modern and powerful army, setting the stage for war.

During the 1930s, the major democracies of the world—including the United States, the United Kingdom, and France—seemed weak and unable to stop the rise of the Axis countries. After World War I, many people

Adolf Hitler (center left) at a Nazi Party meeting in Nuremberg, Germany, in September 1936. Hitler rapidly strengthened the German army in the 1930s.

had strong antiwar feelings. These "protectionists" didn't want their countries involved in a big war once again.

In the United States, President Franklin Roosevelt was busy dealing with the Great Depression. He worried about the aggressive Axis countries, but Congress passed Neutrality Acts that kept Roosevelt from becoming involved in foreign wars.

In the United Kingdom, future Prime Minister Winston Churchill warned people about the Nazi menace and urged the country to build up its armed forces, but few listened.

Adolf Hitler wanted to build a "Greater Germany" that united all German-speaking people into one powerful empire. This included lands lost after World War I. He also wanted to create a racist society that excluded certain people, especially Jews, whom he blamed for many of Germany's problems.

As the 1930s came to an end, events spun out of control. In October 1935, Italy invaded the East African country of Ethiopia. In 1936, civil war broke out in Spain between rebel army forces, led by General Francisco Franco, and the elected government. More than 400,000 people were killed in the war. Franco became the dictator of Spain, thanks in large part to help from Nazi Germany and Fascist Italy.

In 1936, General Francisco Franco led fascist troops against Spain's elected government during the Spanish Civil War. In 1939, he took control of the government and became dictator of Spain.

MARCH 1938

Adolf Hitler rides through the streets of Vienna, Austria, on March 14, 1938, two days after the *Anschluss* forced Austria to become a part of Nazi Germany.

In March 1936, Hitler moved troops into the Rhineland, the western part of Germany that borders France, Luxembourg, and Belgium. It was a violation of the Versailles Treaty, but Great Britain and France did nothing to stop him. In March 1938, he sent troops into German-speaking Austria and took over the country. It was called the *Anschluss* ("link up").

Prime Minister Neville Chamberlain led the United Kingdom. In the hope of avoiding war, he wanted to "appease" Hitler by giving in to many of the dictator's demands.

Chamberlain announces the Munich Agreement signed by himself, Adolf Hitler, Benito Mussolini, and Edouard Daladier (France). It did not keep peace in Europe.

In September 1938, Chamberlain met with Hitler, Mussolini, and other leaders at a conference in Munich, Germany. When he returned to England, he had a signed statement of friendship between his country and Germany. He said the Munich Agreement achieved "peace for our time." Chamberlain would be proven tragically wrong.

Hitler's expansion continued in March 1939 with the invasion of Czechoslovakia and part of Lithuania. After the Czech capital of Prague fell, Great Britain and France pledged support for Poland, the next likely target of Hitler's plan for a Greater Germany.

In August 1939, Germany and the Soviet Union signed a secret "nonaggression" treaty. Each side promised not to attack the other under certain conditions. Hitler no longer had to worry about the powerful Soviet Union blocking his plans for German expansion.

On November 9-10, 1938, the Nazis attacked many Jewish businesses and churches in Germany. The incident is called *Kristallnacht* ("Night of Broken Glass") because of all the shop windows that were shattered. About 30,000 Jews were arrested and sent to concentration camps. In the United States, President Roosevelt condemned the attacks, but there was little he could do. The incident was yet another ominous reason to mistrust Hitler and the rise of Nazi Germany.

During Kristallnacht, many Jewish stores were broken into and looted.

UNITED KINGDOM

NETHERLANDS

BELGIUM

LUX

RHINELAND

GERMANY

GERMANY (EAST PRUSSIA)

POLAND

SUDETENLAND

PROTECTORATE OF BOHEMIA AND MORAVIA

SLOVAKIA

FRANCE

AUSTRIA

SWITZERLAND

HUNGARY

Land controlled by Germany by the end of March 1939.

ITALY

YUGOSLAVIA

The INVASION OF POLAND

World War II officially began on September 1, 1939, the day Germany invaded Poland. For years, Germany had claimed territory in parts of Poland. Now Hitler was determined to take it by force, even though France and the United Kingdom agreed to help Poland if Germany attacked.

The German army, the *Wehrmacht*, used a new kind of fighting style called *blitzkrieg* (lightning warfare). Fast-moving attacks that combined infantry, tanks, and planes smashed through weak spots in the enemy's lines. The shock tactics worked: despite putting up a strong fight, the poorly equipped Polish army was crushed in just a few short weeks.

Polish land was divided between Germany and the Soviet Union, which had also attacked from the east. Poland had a large Jewish population. Millions were killed during the war.

The United Kingdom and France declared war on Germany shortly after the Polish invasion. It did little to stop Hitler's army.

In the United Kingdom, people blamed Prime Minister Chamberlain for the worsening war situation. He resigned, and was replaced by Winston Churchill on May 10, 1940.

German soldiers attack targets in Poland in September 1939.

1939–

MAY

1940

Invasion of
Denmark

Invasion of
Norway

In April 1940, Germany invaded the neutral countries of Denmark and Norway. A helpless Denmark crumbled in a single day. Norway was better prepared, but within two months, it also surrendered.

The FALL OF FRANCE

There was little battlefield action in Western Europe for several months after the German invasion of Poland, despite declarations of war from the United Kingdom and France. In the United States, this period was called the "Phoney War." Many people thought all-out war wouldn't happen at all.

Then, on May 10, 1940, Germany launched its long-awaited attack. German armed forces invaded the neutral countries of Belgium, the Netherlands, and Luxembourg, bypassing a series of border defenses in France called the Maginot Line. It then pushed south into France itself.

At this point in the war, German tanks weren't much better than Allied armor. But the Germans used their forces more effectively. They combined tanks, aircraft, and infantry in rapid strikes that punched holes in the enemy lines.

Many British, French, and Belgian soldiers found themselves surrounded by the Germans, their backs against the English Channel at the French coastal city of Dunkirk. In what is now called the "miracle of Dunkirk," about 340,000 troops were evacuated by a flotilla of ships and small boats to the safety of England.

After Dunkirk, France was quickly overrun, suffering the same fate as Poland. It surrendered in just six weeks. On June 28, 1940, Hitler went sightseeing in the French capital of Paris.

Soldiers in Dunkirk wait for a ship.

Hitler in Paris on June 28, 1940.

MAY – JUNE 1940

15

The AIR BATTLE FOR BRITAIN

After the fall of France, the United Kingdom's Prime Minister Winston Churchill rallied his citizens and warned them of the battle to come. He rejected any kind of peace deal with Germany's Adolf Hitler.

Hitler wanted to send an invasion force across the English Channel—Operation Sea Lion—but it would never work unless Germany controlled the skies. On July 10, 1940, German *Luftwaffe* bombers and fighters began attacking British Royal Air Force (RAF) targets in southern England.

During the Battle of Britain, outnumbered RAF pilots, flying Spitfire and Hurricane fighters and aided by early warning radar, shot down many German planes. Germany was forced to change its tactics and started bombing British cities at night, including the capital of London. Even though "The Blitz" killed tens of thousands of people, the British did not surrender. Germany never gained air superiority, and was forced to call off its invasion plans.

After the Battle of Britain, Winston Churchill praised the brave RAF pilots: "Never in the field of human conflict was so much owed by so many to so few."

German bombers in the air during the Battle of Britain.

Aircraft spotter on the roof of a building in London.

Hurricane planes in flight defending Britain.

JULY 1940–
MAY 1941

OPERATION
BARBAROSSA

Germany surprised the Soviet Union by invading its territory starting on June 22, 1941. Hitler hated communists, and despised the Slavic people. Also, there were many Jews living in the Soviet Union. Hitler wanted to exterminate them all. Plus, the German leader was determined to take the Soviet Union's vast resources for Germany.

The attack was called Operation Barbarossa. With a force of about four million men, the German army shattered the Soviet defenses. But as the months dragged on, winter weather, dwindling supplies, and fierce Soviet resistance stopped the Germans. They were unable to take two major Soviet cities, Moscow and Leningrad.

Fighting was brutal. About 3.5 million Soviet soldiers died by the end of the year, and millions more were captured and later died. The Germans lost about 750,000 men. In addition, millions of civilians were massacred or starved to death. Many Jews were singled out and executed by Nazi SS death squads.

Even though Prime Minister Churchill and President Roosevelt hated communism, they threw their countries' support to Joseph Stalin and the Soviet Union. The three countries formed an alliance in the hope of finally stopping Germany.

18

German soldiers in an armored vehicle approach a burning Russian truck. The invasion of the Soviet Union brought millions of soldiers and civilians into fierce and deadly fighting.

JUNE-DECEMBER

1941

The BATTLE OF THE ATLANTIC

Even before it officially entered the war, the United States provided the United Kingdom and the Soviet Union with critical war supplies. Most of these supplies were sent by large groups of ships called convoys, which were usually escorted by warships.

The German navy sank many Allied merchant ships, especially in the first years of the war. More than 30,000 British sailors were killed during the struggle to control the sea lanes.

On May 27, 1941, after an epic sea battle, the British Royal Navy sank the mighty German battleship *Bismarck*. It was a great boost to Allied morale.

German submarines (called U-boats) hunted in groups called "wolf packs." They were

A German U-boat surfaces near the coast of northern France in 1940.

very effective at striking their targets with torpedoes and then disappearing under the ocean.

By the spring of 1943, the tide turned against the Germans. The Allies, now equipped with sonar, depth charges, air patrols, and submarines of their own, decimated Germany's U-boat fleet.

1939–1945

A German U-boat crew watches the sinking of a torpedoed tanker in 1942.

The EMPIRE OF JAPAN

Just as Germany and Italy wanted to expand their power, the military leaders of Japan had dreams of their own Asian empire. In July 1937, Japan invaded a fractured and weak China. Some of the worst fighting took place in the port city of Shanghai. In September 1940, Japan officially became part of the Axis alliance, along with Nazi Germany and Fascist Italy. The United States was very alarmed. It began building a powerful fleet of U.S. Navy ships that it could use to counter Japan's aggression.

Japan moved troops into French Indochina in 1940 and 1941. Fearing a takeover of American and European economic interests in Asia, the United States demanded that Japan withdraw its troops. Japan ignored the Americans. In response, the United States blocked the sale of critical trade goods to Japan, including oil.

At that time, Japan received about 80 percent of its oil from the United States. The American oil embargo was seen by many in the Japanese military as a declaration of war.

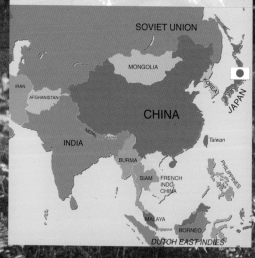

The Japanese army bombed and then occupied the city of Nanking in December 1937. Approximately 300,000 Chinese civilians were massacred. The Japanese eventually occupied much of the north and east of China, but didn't achieve a complete victory.

1937–1945

The ATTACK ON PEARL HARBOR

Japan wanted to cripple the United States' Pacific Fleet. Japanese military leaders hoped that by the time America rebuilt its navy, Japan would have such a strong hold on Asia that no country could stop it.

On the morning of December 7, 1941, more than 350 Japanese planes from six aircraft carriers attacked the United States naval base at Pearl Harbor, Hawaii. The Americans were totally surprised. Japanese Kate torpedo bombers and Val dive bombers sank or destroyed 18 U.S. warships. The biggest loss was the USS *Arizona*, which exploded and killed almost 1,200 men. Japanese Zero fighters also destroyed about 200 American aircraft. Luckily, American aircraft carriers were at sea at the time, and escaped the devastation.

The Japanese attack on the naval base at Pearl Harbor lasted barely 90 minutes. Approximately 2,400 Americans were killed, and another 1,100 wounded.

Admiral Yamamoto was the chief planner of the Pearl Harbor attack. He correctly believed in the new power of naval aircraft carriers.

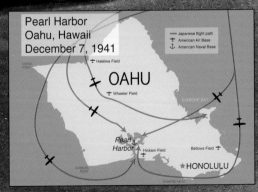

Pearl Harbor
Oahu, Hawaii
December 7, 1941

Japanese flight path
American Air Base
American Naval Base

KAENA POINT
† Haleiwa Field
OAHU
† Wheeler Field
KANEOHE BAY
Pearl Harbor
Hickam Field
Bellows Field †
BARBERS POINT
★ HONOLULU
DIAMOND HEAD

DECEMBER 7
1941

25

The attack at Pearl Harbor occurred before Japan had declared war. Since the United States and Japan were officially at peace, the surprise attack enraged Americans. In the years to come, "Remember Pearl Harbor!" was a frequently heard phrase used to rally the American people.

One day after the Japanese attack, President Roosevelt addressed the United States Congress. He called December 7, 1941, a "date which will live in infamy." Congress immediately declared war on Japan.

Germany's Adolf Hitler, in support of his Japanese ally, declared war on the United States on December 11. Italy's Benito Mussolini also declared war. The United States then declared war on both Germany and Italy.

President Roosevelt addressed Congress on December 8, 1941, at 12:30 p.m., asking them to declare war on Japan. Within hours, Congress passed, and Roosevelt signed, a formal Declaration of War.

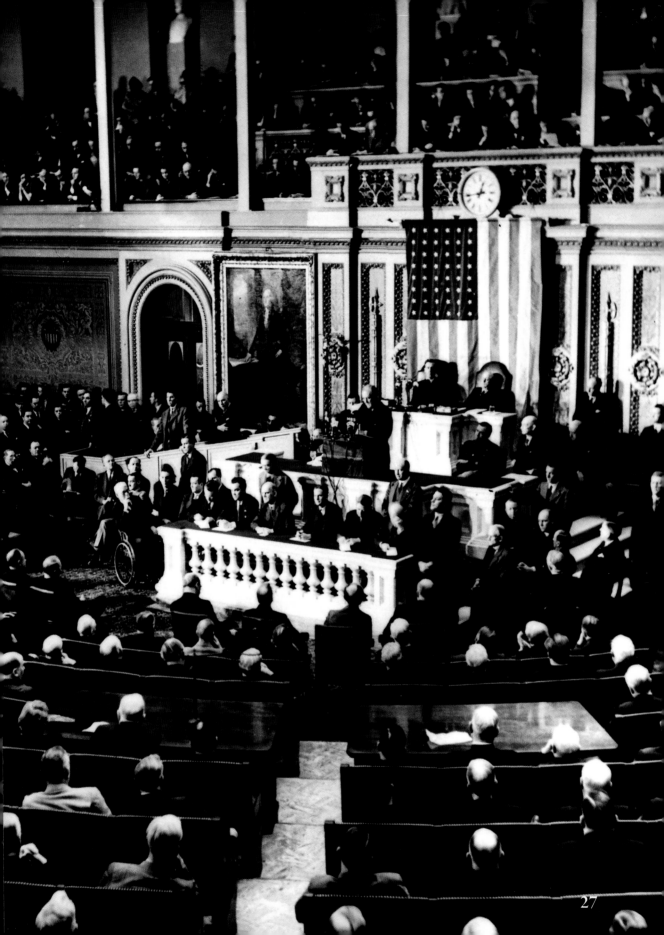

JAPANESE VICTORIES

To gain the oil, rubber, and other natural resources for its expanding empire, Japan launched a series of attacks on countries in Southeast Asia and the Central Pacific. The ferocious attacks were well planned, combining naval and air power with ground troops who were fanatically dedicated to Emperor Hirohito and the Japanese leadership.

Within six short months, Japan invaded Malaya, Singapore, Burma, Hong Kong, the Dutch East Indies, New Guinea, and the Philippines. Australia and British-held India were also threatened.

In the Philippines, most of American General Douglas MacArthur's army was captured by the Japanese by May 1942.

MacArthur escaped to Australia, vowing to someday return to free the Philippines.

Despite their rapid gains, Japanese forces were stretched thin over an area thousands of miles wide. And across the Pacific, the United States was thirsty for revenge. It trained millions of fresh soldiers, and its enormous industrial capacity began producing a tidal wave of new ships, planes, guns, and bombs for the war ahead.

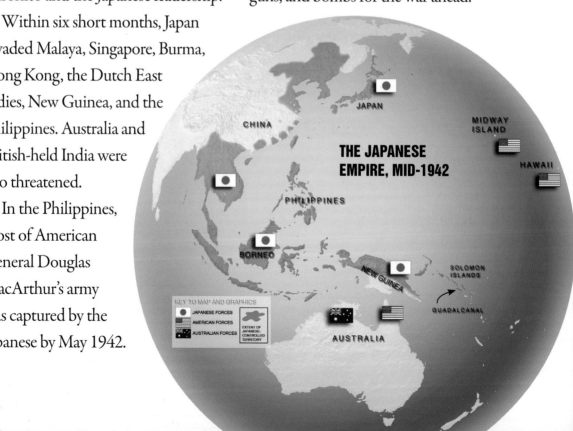

THE JAPANESE EMPIRE, MID-1942

CHINA
JAPAN
MIDWAY ISLAND
HAWAII
PHILIPPINES
BORNEO
NEW GUINEA
SOLOMON ISLANDS
GUADALCANAL
AUSTRALIA

KEY TO MAP AND GRAPHICS

JAPANESE FORCES
AMERICAN FORCES
AUSTRALIAN FORCES
EXTENT OF JAPANESE-CONTROLLED TERRITORY

Japanese soldiers celebrate their victory in the Philippines in April 1942.

GLOSSARY

Air Raid

The dropping of bombs from a military aircraft aimed at a city, factory, or other specific target on the ground.

Allies

The Allies were the many nations that were allied, or joined, in the fight against Germany, Italy, and Japan in World War II. The most powerful nations among the Allies included the United States, the United Kingdom, the Soviet Union, France, China, Canada, and Australia.

Axis

The Axis powers were the World War II alliance of Germany, Italy, and Japan.

Blitzkrieg

A German word meaning "lightning warfare." *Blitzkrieg* called for very large invasions to overwhelm the enemy quickly with combined land and air attacks in order to avoid long, drawn-out battles.

Communism

The Soviet Union was ruled by members of a political party called the Communist Party. Communism is a form of socialism that seeks to abolish classes in society, and to get rid of private ownership such as land or businesses. All individuals are supposed to be equal, and everyone shares in the work according to their abilities. The government has total control over the economy, and restricts personal freedoms.

Fascist

A type of governmental rule where there is one powerful ruler or dictator who uses military might to ensure that all people obey.

GREAT DEPRESSION

The Great Depression was a period of severe economic downturn, starting in 1929 and lasting about a decade. During the Great Depression, jobs were scarce, manufacturing plants were closed, and few people had extra money.

NAZI

The Nazi Party was the political party in Germany that supported Adolf Hitler. After 1934 it was the only political party allowed in Germany. This is when Hitler became a dictator and ruled Germany with total power.

SS

A Nazi secret police organization originally created to be Adolf Hitler's bodyguard. The initials SS stand for the German word *schutzstaffen*, which means "protection squad." As the war progressed, the SS was placed in charge of concentration camps and the extermination of Jewish people.

VERSAILLES TREATY

At the end of World War I (1914-1918), the victorious Allied Powers, including the United Kingdom, France, and the United States, imposed on Germany a set of rules called the Versailles Treaty. It restricted how big an army Germany could have. It also required Germany to give "reparation" money to the Allies to pay for the war. The restrictions placed on Germany were excessive, and did not result in the intended lasting peace. Instead, it led to severe German economic hardship and resentment, which eventually led to World War II. The Versailles Treaty is named after Versailles, France, a suburb of Paris, where the document was created.

WORLD WAR I

A war that was fought in Europe from 1914 to 1918, involving countries around the world. Great Britain, France, Russia, and Italy (the Allies) opposed the Central Powers (Germany, Austria-Hungary, Turkey, and Bulgaria). The United States entered the war in April 1917 on the side of the Allies.

INDEX